Breaking the Chains of Influence: Persuasion Reloaded

By
Greg J. Bayer

2

TABLE OF CONTENTS

INTRODUCTION

A company cannot function on its own. There are numerous elements outside the workplace boundaries that can influence its performance. New technology and changes in taxes, interest rates, or minimum wages are two examples. These are referred to as external forces in business. Continue reading to learn how external variables affect business and how businesses can adapt to an ever-changing external environment.

Business decisions are influenced by two sorts of factors: internal and external. Internal factors are elements that originate within or are under the control of a corporation, such as human resources, organizational structure, corporate culture, and so on. External factors, on the other hand, are forces that originate outside of the organization, such as competition, new technology, and government legislation.

External influences on business
External variables affecting company are classified into five categories:

Political, economic, social, technological, and environmental competitiveness.

Political influences on business

New legislation that affects the rights of consumers, employees, and enterprises is referred to as political influence on business.

Here are some instances of business-related legislation:
- Anti-discrimination
- Intellectual property rights
- The minimum wage
- Health and security
- Competition
- Consumer defense.

These are often classified into three types:

- Consumer laws - These are regulations that require firms to offer excellent goods and services to their customers.
  Employment laws protect employee rights and govern the relationship between employees and customers.
- Intellectual property law - These are the laws that protect creative output in the business

world, such as music, books, films, and software copyrights.

- Economic influences on business
Businesses and the economy are inextricably linked. Business success leads to a healthy economy, whereas a strong economy permits enterprises to grow more quickly. As a result, economic changes will have a considerable impact on business development.

Changes in tax rates can have a significant impact on economic activity.
- Unemployment
- Rates of interest
- Inflation

Social influences on business

Changes in customer tastes, behavior, or attitude that affect business sales and revenues are referred to as social factors affecting business. Consumers, for example, are more concerned about environmental issues such as climate change and pollution. This puts pressure on businesses to develop environmentally friendly production and waste disposal methods.

Social impact also encompasses a company's ethical practices, such as how it treats its employees, customers, and suppliers.

An ethical company respects the needs of all shareholders, not only the owners. Typically, business ethics consists of three major components:
- Employees - Ensure work-life balance as well as employees' physical and emotional well-being.
- Suppliers - Stick to the agreed-upon contract and pay suppliers on time.
- Customers - Offer high-quality goods at reasonable prices. Businesses should not deceive customers or sell things that are harmful to them.

Business and technological factors
Technology is widely used in modern companies, from production to product sales and customer service. Technology enables a company to save time and labor expenses while increasing efficiency, which can result in a competitive advantage in the long run.
Automation, e-commerce, and digital media are three significant aspects of technology in business.

CHAPTER ONE

The Six Principles of Influence

Reciprocity, commitment or consistency, consensus or social proof, authority, like, and scarcity are the six principles of influence.

More than three decades after the book's release, its six ideas have been applied to Internet marketing, particularly the conversion rate company.

1. Reciprocity: Give something in exchange for something in return.

According to the first persuasive principle, we are hardwired to return favors and repay debts—to treat others as they have treated us.

According to the concept of reciprocity, people are naturally obligated to grant discounts or concessions to others if they have received favors from those same people. Psychology explains this by emphasizing that humans despise feeling obligated to others.

In the workplace, you can apply the concept of reciprocity by doing favors for others, assisting others, publicly complimenting others, and overall functioning in such a way that you build up a bank of social responsibilities owed to you. Each of these duties will be met at some point, most likely to your benefit. Of course, if you go too far with this type of conduct, it will stop working.

2. Scarcity

People want something more when there is less of it. This holds true for both material products and experiences. About this one, not much more can be stated.

From a persuasion and influence standpoint, this means that lowering the availability of your product or service (or at least generating a sense of scarcity) may benefit you in increasing interest in it. This principle is evident in a variety of markets. For example, "only 5 seats left at this price" is a typical phrase on online sales platforms for hotels and flights. They do this to instill a sense of scarcity (along with time constraint, which is closely connected). Companies in the consumer goods sector also produce "limited edition" goods. They do this with anything from hand soap to shoes, increasing scarcity by limiting availability.

It is possible to create a sense of scarcity around your own availability in the workplace. This may enhance interest in what you have to offer. Of course, only those in positions of power are in a position to do so. Doing so when you lack that power may merely lead to others accusing you of inefficiency.

3. Authority : You will obey me.
People who are authoritative, credible, and competent professionals in their professions have more influence and persuasiveness than those who are not. Part of the rationale for this is that authority and credibility are fundamental components of trust. We are more prone to follow someone we trust.
Have you ever wondered why we have a tendency to obey authoritative persons even when they are disagreeable and ask others to conduct objectionable acts? It's just human nature.

In actuality, promoting one's own genius and authority is less effective than having others do it for them. Surprisingly, it doesn't seem to matter who that other person is. Even if the person promoting you is known to benefit personally from doing so, their words of encouragement improve your impact and persuasiveness.

In the workplace, this indicates that while trust and credibility are crucial, it is also feasible to get part of that power through the recommendations and kind words of others. It may be worthwhile to ask others to suggest you, or to recommend others so that they feel obligated to recommend you in return.

4. Commitment: People want their views to match their values.
The concept of commitment asserts that humans have a strong desire to be perceived as constant. As a result, once we've publicly committed to something or someone, we're considerably more inclined to follow through (thus, consistency).
This can be explained psychologically by the fact that people have associated commitment with their self-image. Marketers, of course, have discovered how to apply this second concept to increase conversion rates.

They improve the possibility that site visitors will eventually consider themselves as clients by encouraging them to commit to something relatively little (and usually free), such as a guide or whitepaper. That shift in self-perception makes it easier to follow up with a paid product or service offer. (This is comparable to the "foot in the door" method.)
Surprisingly, once someone gives you a favor, they identify as the type of person who does you favors and are more inclined to do so again in the future.

This means that if you convince someone to do you a tiny favor (like lend you a pen or buy you a cup of coffee), they are more likely to do you another favor in the future. Of course, no matter how you choose to interact with and with others, you must live with yourself.

5. Liking: The more you like someone, the more likely you are to be convinced by them.
How much of a difference does like someone make?

It influences your odds of being affected by that person. Liking is based on a similarity or a more superficial interest, such as physical appeal.
This notion is frequently seen in the worlds of marketing and advertising. Almost every advertising you encounter will include people who are intended to appeal to the product's target market. The consumer is more likely to be affected by someone with whom they associate and like.

To apply this approach in the workplace, you just need to become liked by those around you as well as those you want to persuade or influence. You can accomplish this by collaborating with others, providing genuine praises to others, discovering similarities, and developing relationships. The crucial point here is that you must first establish these relationships and gain this "liking" before attempting to influence others. If you strive to become loved after you've begun your influence efforts, those efforts will fail.

6. Social Proof: Humans are social beings who believe it is vital to comply with the standards of a social group. This means that while making decisions, we frequently look around to check what others are doing before making our own. Nothing beats feeling affirmed by what others are doing. Social proof is defined as people doing what they see others doing. There is safety in numbers.
For example, if our coworkers work late, we are more likely to do the same. We are more likely to try a restaurant if it is consistently crowded.
This idea has an even greater impact on us if: we are insecure about ourselves. The people we observe appear to be similar to ourselves.

There are numerous experiments in social psychology that demonstrate this inherent human phenomena, but a famous example is this 1960s elevator.
If the group looks to the back of the elevator, the individual will do the same, even if it appears

strange. Most people refuse to think or act on their own.

Finally, For decades, corporations and marketers have utilized these six principles of influence to persuade you, the customer, to part with your hard-earned money.

Six principles have been established since the rise of ecommerce.
Keep these concepts in mind at all times. Learn about them and how to use them on your website. Don't be hesitant to offer a free sample or two to potential customers, and definitely let them know if your products won't be accessible for long or at specific costs.

CHAPTER TWO

Understanding the Psychology of Influence

The notion that people may be convinced to do things is the foundation of influence in psychology. A lot of the time, influence is an accidental act. It works because people are frequently oblivious when they are being impacted.

Many people want to feel like they belong and yet stand out from the crowd. They feel comfortable making decisions they think will make them fit in or be popular with others.

People find it difficult to decide a lot of the time. Making the wrong choices can waste time and money and damage your reputation.

Thorough study and being aware of every facet of your decision are necessary for making a successful decision. Finding the time and energy to consistently make the required effort can be challenging, though.

One way to avoid making a mistake is to heed the advice of others. In general, people are more likely to heed the counsel of a respected friend or an authority figure.

Understanding the psychology of influence, brands work with influencers to draw in and win over their target audience.

Although the psychology of influence is not a novel concept, its applications have changed, especially with regard to influencer marketing.
A cognitive bias is a systematic mistake in cognition that arises as people take in and process information from their environment, which then shapes their conclusions and decisions.
Although the human brain is incredibly strong, it is not without limitations. Often, the brain's attempt to streamline information processing results in cognitive biases. Biases are commonly employed as general guidelines to aid in understanding the world and hastening decision-making.

There are biases connected to memory. Your recollection of an event could be skewed for a number of reasons, which could result in skewed judgment and thinking.
Attention problems may be associated with other cognitive biases. Since attention is a limited resource, people need to be selective about what they focus on in their environment.

Consequently, little prejudices may creep in and affect your perspective and way of thinking about the world.

Symptoms of Cognitive Bias
All people possess cognitive biases. It is important to realize that it affects your thinking as well, even though it might be simpler to identify in others. The following are some signs that a cognitive bias could be affecting you:

- Focusing only on news articles that support your opinions
- When things don't work out as planned, you assign blame to other factors.
- Assuming that everyone else thinks the same as you Doing things the way you do and attributing other people's success to luck
- Having only a cursory knowledge of a subject and then assuming you are an expert on it
- You would rather think that you are unbiased, reasonable, and able to process and evaluate all pertinent data while you are passing judgment on and making decisions about the world around you. Regretfully, these prejudices may lead us to draw incorrect inferences and conclusions.

Types of Cognitive Bias

Find out more about some of the most common kinds of cognitive biases that can skew the way you think.

Actor-observer bias is the propensity to attribute internal causes to other people's behaviors while attributing external causes to your own actions. For instance, you might attribute your high cholesterol to heredity while criticizing others for eating poorly and not exercising.

The tendency to place undue emphasis on the first piece of information you acquire is known as anchoring bias. If you discover, for instance, that a car typically costs a certain amount, you might think that any sum below that is a fantastic deal and stop searching for a better deal. You can take advantage of this tendency and influence other people's expectations by presenting the first information for consideration.

The propensity to give certain objects attention while ignoring others is known as attentional bias. For instance, you might look at the outside and interior design of an automobile while ignoring its safety record and gas mileage.

The availability heuristic highlights the significance of knowledge that is instantly recalled. You tend to overestimate the likelihood that similar events will occur in the future and to put more faith in this information.

The propensity to accept facts that contradicts your preconceived notions while favoring information that supports them is known as confirmation bias.
The false consensus effect is the tendency to overestimate how much other people agree with you.
The inclination to believe that something can only be used in one way is known as functional fixedness. For instance, you might not think about driving a nail into the wall with a big wrench if you don't have a hammer. If you don't have a cork board to tack items to, you might think you don't need thumbtacks, but you should think about the other uses for them. This could also apply to the roles that people play, like not realizing that a personal assistant has the potential to be a leader.

The phenomenon known as the "halo effect" happens when your general perception of someone affects your feelings and thoughts about them. This is particularly true of their physical appeal, which affects your evaluation of their other qualities.

The misinformation effect is the propensity for information learned after an event to cloud memories of the original event. It is easy for what you learn about the incident from other people to interfere with your memory. It has the effect of making people doubt eyewitness testimony.

An emphasis on positivity Because of this bias, you believe that you have a higher chance of success and are less likely to be unlucky than your peers.
The tendency to assign responsibility for positive outcomes and take credit for negative ones is known as self-serving bias. For instance, in a poker game, success comes from knowing the odds and reading the other players, whereas losing comes from getting dealt a poor hand.

When someone believes they are more intelligent and capable than they actually are, it's known as the Dunning-Kruger effect. For example, when they are unable to recognize their own shortcomings.
Sometimes, you may act and think differently due to a combination of prejudices. As an illustration, the misinformation effect may cause you to recall an incident incorrectly and lead you to assume that everyone else does as well (the false consensus effect).

Bias Elements

Even the easiest choice would take a long time to make if you had to take into account every possible option. It's common to rely on mental shortcuts that let you behave quickly due to the complexity of the world around you and the volume of information available.

Though there are many other factors that might lead to cognitive biases, heuristics—or mental shortcuts—often play a major part. Though sometimes remarkably accurate, they can occasionally result in cognitive errors.

The following are other elements that may exacerbate these biases:

- Sentiment
- Individual reasons
- Information processing limitations in the mind
- Social compulsive behaviors

Because cognitive flexibility declines with aging, cognitive bias may also increase.

The Impact of Cognitive Dissonance

Thinking errors can be caused by cognitive biases. Conspiracy theories, for instance, tend to be influenced by a variety of biases. Cognitive biases are not necessarily harmful, though. Psychologists claim that many of these biases have an adaptive function since they help us make snap decisions. This is particularly crucial in situations where there is danger or threat.

The Effect of Social Identity on Our Perspectives, Sentiments, and Activities

Have you at any point contemplated the impact that social Identity has? It provides us with a feeling of local area and having a place, and it impacts our mentalities, feelings, and activities in manners we probably won't actually know about. Our social characters — whether they come from a typical political philosophy or an affection for sports groups — significantly affect how we see ourselves and draw in with the world.

We'll look at the fascinating subject of social character in this blog entry, alongside its benefits and disservices, and give direction on fostering a positive identity inside your own informal communities. Presently we should examine the impact of social personality! Simply stand by till you perceive how acquisition is involved assuming that you're asking what it has to do with any of this

What is Social Identity precisely?

The piece of our self-idea that outcomes from being an individual from a specific gathering is known as our social Identity. It is predicated on how we see shared convictions, interests, or attributes — like orientation or race — among ourselves and others. Our feeling of association and reason in life is gotten from our feeling of having a place with specific associations. Being encircled by individuals who share our encounters or perspectives frequently brings us solace. For example, you could feel closer to other people who share major areas of strength for you for ecological backing assuming you have overwhelming inclinations toward sustainability.

Social Identity can have both positive and negative components. From one perspective, it can give us an internal compass and a feeling of help from the local area when we face difficulties. However, it could likewise bring about bias against others beyond our own interpersonal organizations.

It's vital to remember that social characters advance as we cooperate with new people and have new encounters. By recognizing this versatility, we can attempt to make positive, comprehensive social personalities that advance incorporation as opposed to prohibition.

What makes obtainment vital, then? Like some other industry or field, acquisition has its own arrangement of convictions and values that shape the social personalities of the people who work in it. How does our Social Identity impact the manner in which we think, feel, and act?

Social Identity assumes a huge part in our lives since it shapes the manner in which we view ourselves and others. Our social Identities are molded by the various gatherings we are a piece of, including our families, companions, societies, religions, and even side interests.

Our social Identity shapes our convictions since it gives us a sensation of motivation and having a place. It is human instinct for us to embrace the convictions and upsides of other people who are like us. This might lead us to support explicit causes or ideas since they line up with the upsides of our own gathering.

Social Identity has a profound effect too since we experience responsibility when something pessimistic happens and pride when our gathering succeeds. These sentiments might impact our connections with other people who are not individuals from our gathering.

Behavior is one area in which social Identity has the most effect. People having a place with various gatherings might experience predisposition and segregation because of contrasts in race, orientation, sexual direction, or religion, which might make them change their lead as needs be.

Our social Identities impact our self-insight as well as our social communications with others. Understanding oneself is an important initial move toward perceiving inclinations inside oneself and making a move to further develop society.

Emotional Appeal's Power

The objective of involving profound requests in showcasing is to lay out a cozy connection between the client and the organization. By speaking to clients' feelings, advertisers can make a feeling of significance, criticalness, and association.

Emotional appeals that inspire sensations of dread, happiness, love, or sentimentality are only a couple of the numerous that advertisers can utilize. Each kind of close to home allure works by speaking to the interest group's different longings and feelings.

For example, dread requests are usually utilized in general wellbeing efforts to advance change in conduct. Emotional and horrifying symbolism is at times utilized in these ads to delineate the results of sitting idle, for example, the dangers related with smoking or unprotected sex.

On the other hand, to construct areas of strength for a with the organization, satisfaction and love requests are generally utilized in way of life and purchaser promotion. Delightful symbolism, elevating messages, and agreeable music are generally utilized in these advertisements to complement the brand's good implications.

In marketing, emotional appeals function best when they make an association between the customer and the brand. By playing on their feelings, advertisers might cause their crowd to feel pertinent and dire. Advertisers that comprehend the many kinds of close to home requests and how they work can make viable commercials that associate with their main interest group.

CHAPTER THREE

Using Influence in Sales and Marketing

In sales, influence involves taking the lead and masterfully directing a customer along the buying path, ultimately arriving at a conclusion that is in their benefit as well as yours.

It's a subtle process that the customer may not notice until the end, when they realize how much you've contributed to an interesting, informative, and intelligent buying decision.

Sales is about assisting individuals in moving from their existing state to a new and better place, their new reality. It all comes down to change in the end. When you make the case for change and motivate people to act, you influence them.

Your value proposition assists you in making the case for change. What you're selling must resonate with the buyer, distinguish itself as the finest option among all other possibilities, and your claims must be validated.

In other words, if done well, customers will say to themselves, "I need this," "It's the best choice," and "I believe in this seller, offering, company, and outcome."

However, making the value case is not enough. You must also motivate buyers to take action.

If you are successful, the buyer will have a high level of trust in the purchasing decision. The buyer is more likely to be your internal stakeholder champion. The buyer is inspired to act on his or her confidence and complete the purchase. You are more likely to obtain these results if you enhance your influence with buyers.

Marketing can assist sales by developing call collateral, developing websites that complement and accelerate the sales cycle, and raising brand awareness so salespeople can focus on the benefits of their product or service rather than wasting time describing what it is in the first place.

In brief, marketing's role is to expedite sales and take consumers through the buyer's journey as swiftly and easily as possible.

This is especially true as the team in charge of each stage of the sales funnel changes. Traditionally, marketing would make prospects aware of and interested in their product or service, and sales would help those prospects decide whether or not to purchase it.

However, especially in the post-pandemic era, individuals prefer to educate themselves rather than rely on a salesperson to instruct them. That is why it is a modern marketing team's responsibility to not only make prospects aware, but also to assist them educate themselves, ensure that they are ready to make a buy, and work with their choice to go with the advertiser's organization.

A comparison graph of the conventional and current marketing funnels

In turn, a sales team may assist marketing by sharing field information about prospects and clients, providing feedback on whether strategies and campaigns are effective, and coordinating on the brand story they're telling during meetings.

How can you increase your sales influence?

To actively establish and enhance your sales impact, apply the 11 Principles of impact.
1. Create a chasm between the buyer's current situation and their new reality. A Buyer Change

Blueprint is the most effective way to visually express this difference. This allows you to demonstrate both the intellectual (return on investment) rationale for change and the emotional urge for action.

2. Be approachable. People who they like buy from, listen to, and trust.

3. Encourage ownership. The more a buyer believes they own the agenda and want to change it, the more likely they are to proceed with the process.

4. Establish the rational explanation for the transaction by making the justification case. The need to rationalize each decision is part of the human experience.

5. Emphasize your distinctions. If you actually have something original, groundbreaking, or significantly different from others, you will have a much simpler job distinguishing yourself from the competitors. In most cases, the difference is you, the vendor, and the value you bring.

6. Encourage scarcity. When a consumer believes something is scarce, he or she wants it even more.

7. Develop the buyer's trust and belief in four crucial areas:

The buyer has faith in and confidence in you as a seller.
The buyer is certain that your items or services will perform as promised.
The buyer believes the company is a good fit.
The buyer feels the outcome will be realized in a reasonable amount of time.

8. Be unconcerned. Accept the possibility of losing this sale. Accept the possibility of moving on to other chances. Having the confidence and desire to walk away can help you save time, avoid appearing dependent, and may even motivate a buyer to move further.

9. Create a sense of urgency. People don't enjoy missing out, and if they think they might, they tend to move more swiftly.

10. Make use of stepping stones. To move the process along, take little measures. People are significantly more likely to stay on a course once they start.

11. Encourage dedication. When people make vocal, written, and public commitments, they are more likely to keep them.

Sales-Increase Marketing Strategies

1. Direct Marketing
   Using an outbound marketing strategy, reach out to customers and meet them where they are. This is traditional marketing; it involves putting your brand in front of those who aren't actively looking for it.
   When your desired audience is unaware that a solution to their pain points exists, or you need to see results quickly, this marketing method is beneficial for driving sales.

2. Content Marketing
   An inbound marketing strategy is the inverse of outbound marketing. It boosts sales by guaranteeing that those looking for exactly what you have to offer can discover you. By focusing on education, you can even help individuals who need you but don't realize it finds you. Nobody likes being sold to, but when done correctly, inbound marketing allows your customers to sell themselves on your products and services.

- Remember the new marketing and sales funnel. This marketing plan is tailored to it, with assets that assist consumers in becoming aware of the answer to their problem, considering your brand, and deciding whether or not to purchase.

3. Customized Marketing
Nobody wants to be treated like a number. This is when personalized marketing comes into play. 80% of consumers are more inclined to buy from a firm that provides a personalized experience, and 72% will not engage with your marketing unless it is personalized. And sales do improve when you use this marketing method.

To be ultra-specific in who you target with your messaging, this method combines inbound and outbound tactics, as well as extensive research and audience segmentation. This makes it more complex than other marketing methods, however automation and other MarTech tools can help you simplify these procedures so that they are doable even for small and medium-sized businesses.

4. **User-Generated/Third-Party**
   Content Customer acquisition is especially tough because sales and marketing are among the least trusted professions today. Whereas your audience once relied on you for information and education, they now actively disregard everything a business has to say.

   As a result, concentrating on what others are saying about your company through case studies and testimonials on your site, as well as user reviews and press mentions on other sites, can be a successful marketing technique for increasing sales. Instead of pressing your message on someone who may or may not be interested, simply highlight delighted consumers.

5. **Concentrate on the Brand Story**
   Your salespeople aren't performing sales activities until they present a prospect with a contract; they're the most valuable marketing your company has. They reach out to your target demographic, customize their message, keep the brand at the forefront of their minds, and more. As a result, aligning both teams is one of the most cost-effective

and important marketing methods a company can do to enhance sales.

This is a strategy rather than a tactic because it is continual, always evolving, and requires several deliverables to be adequately executed. By ensuring that leadership agrees on the focus of your brand and that their teams are all communicating the same story in client meetings, on a well-designed website, and elsewhere, you make your business clear and accessible to customers.

Developing Effective Persuasive Messaging

A Sale communication is a persuasive message intended to persuade the recipient to take the desired action (often, to make a purchase) in relation to the value proposition supplied by the sender. We are most familiar with pitches designed to persuade a customer to buy a product or use a service.

The structure of the sales message will differ based on whether the communication was solicited or requested by the recipient (for example, when you contact a company for product information) or unsolicited (for example, a cold call or postal advertisement).

You want to build up to the sales pitch in the latter scenario, thus an inductive message is acceptable. It allows you to deliver persuasive aspects prior to making a call to action (buying request).

A deductive message is more acceptable if the communication was requested. Essentially, you supply the customer with the required information without first providing supporting information.

AIDA is a frequent technique for persuading someone to make a purchase. As such, it is essentially an unsolicited communication, resulting in an inductive message structure.

The acronym AIDA describes;
Obtain the attention of the receiver.
Arousal of interest upon the launch of a product.
Making room for the product's desire by pitching its value to the receivers.
Motivate people to take action.

Using Social Proof to Increase Customer Satisfaction

Social proof is a significant psychological phenomena that impacts how clients see and interface with items, administrations, and brands. It alludes to individuals' proclivity to copy the demonstrations, thoughts, or suggestions of others, especially those they trust or appreciate. Here, you will find how to use social proof in your showcasing efforts to affect shopper conduct and navigation.

What is the meaning of social proof in Marketing?

Social proof is a significant part of advertising since it might help foster trust and believability, influence feelings and perspectives, and inspire activities and changes. Positive criticism, affirmation, or acknowledgment from others can decrease a buyer's distrust or vulnerability, while speaking to their convictions, desires, or identities can fortify their close to home association with your brand. Besides, social proof that shows the advantages, impacts, or results of using an item or administration could convince buyers to go with a buy decision.

What role does social proof play in your marketing campaigns?

To involve social proof in your promoting efforts, you should initially comprehend your ideal interest group's requests, then select the suitable structure and wellspring of social proof, show it unmistakably and decisively, then test and enhance it. You can find out about your crowd's preferences and ways of behaving by utilizing studies, interviews, examinations, or personas. You can use client created material, master authority, social approval, or FOMO relying upon your item or administration and the phase of the purchaser's excursion. It is basic to situate your social proof where your crowd can rapidly see it and where it can easily affect their direction.

To survey the viability of your social proof, you can use A/B testing, input, or examination devices. You might build the unwavering quality and persuasiveness of your brand by utilizing social evidence in an intelligent way and really.

How can one use influence if most sales are set up as total strangers?

Simple: cultivate relationships with prominent people. You'll need someone with clout to set up your appointments. For example, if you offer "key man" or "buy/sell" life insurance to business owners, establish a relationship with a business attorney. As the business attorney drafts partnership agreements that require "buy/sell" life insurance, the attorney refers you to the insurance company to resolve the issue. You now have a powerful individual recommending you to write their life insurance. Building relationships is essential for a successful sales career.

CHAPTER FOUR

Personal Relationship Influence

Relationships are just easier to build with individuals you experience every now and again since you have the chance to get to know them.
One more angle that figures out who we develop relationships with is likeness. We are more disposed to become companions or darlings with individuals who have similar foundations, perspectives, and ways of life to us. Social bonds can impart a feeling of obligation and worry for other people, which can prompt people participating in ways of behaving that defend both the strength of others and their own. Social ties give data and lay out standards that influence wellbeing ways of behaving.

Figuring out how to improve your relationships can help both your expert and individual lives. This ability will help you whether you need to feel more associated with your sweetheart or have a superior relationship with your boss.

We as a whole need individuals who mean quite a bit to us to realize that we give it a second thought: our dearest friends, relatives, and colleagues. Yet, occasionally, we sense the connection dissolving. We might lose contact for a period or become excessively centered around ourselves. Regardless of whether we see somebody consistently, fostering major areas of strength requires exertion.

There are little things you can do to show somebody you give it a second thought, for example, purchasing blossoms for your accomplice or some espresso for your most loved colleague. In any case, if you really need to make that relationship more significant, you should put in any amount of work.

Further developing your correspondence capacities is the most important move toward extending an association. It likewise requires that you work in such a way that helps everybody's prosperity. Getting to realize somebody may be troublesome, yet there could be no more excellent time than now to begin figuring out how to reinforce your relationships.

42

What is the significance of connections in our emotional well-being?

You don't need to be a people person to comprehend the reason why relationships are significant. Relationships empower us to pay attention to other people and their perspectives. Our relationships likewise offer us solace when we really want it and help us in managing life's burdens.

Expect you've been annoyed by something and don't have the foggiest idea how to determine it. Your closest friend could help you in settling your trouble by giving a position or relationship prompt. You can deal with your interests together. You can likewise basically request that a companion confirm your sentiments when important.

Relationships likewise urge us to care more for ourselves and focus on our wellbeing. Individuals who care about you might perceive when you are battling and offer you their help.
They care more about your prosperity than any other individual's. Besides, investing quality energy with your buddies advises you that you are cherished, which eases feelings of separation and dejection.

The more prominent the profundity of the relationship, the bigger the prizes.
Constructing and supporting sound relationships is a fundamental component of keeping up with our psychological well-being.

The following are six remarkable ideas to assist you with yours.

1. Get to know yourself
Get some margin to adore yourself and associate with your feelings so you might articulate your thoughts plainly and really.
Not knowing how to control your feelings and express them in a sound manner could negatively affect your emotional wellness.

2. Set forth the energy and exertion
Sound relationships are made as opposed to found.
A sound relationship requires responsibility and an eagerness to oblige each other's necessities.

3.Establish and adhere to boundaries
Defining limits is tied in with conveying not just what you don't need or like in your connections, yet additionally about telling everyone around you what you esteem.

Consider and convey your limits to other people, for example, regarding your alone time.
This alleviates the tension on your relationship to focus on anything ridiculous.

4. Communicate and Listen

Conflicts are typical in all relationships. It is important that you pay attention to and speak with one another. Focus on seeing instead of responding. Make it a point to discuss your thoughts or weaknesses with those you trust.

5. Give up control

Quite a bit of life is around how we answer our encounters and experiences. Realizing that you can handle what you do and not what others truly do can save you investment.

6. Consider and learn

You can respond to others' sentiments in a solid manner in the event that you have a sound technique for communicating your own. Being angry at somebody much of the time originates from a position of harmed and vexed. on the off chance that you can perceive that, you can impart it, and foster more grounded associations with others.

Changing Family Interactions and Dynamics

Elements are powers that can influence or frame a framework. Relationship elements are those communications between people that decide their thought process of each other, what they do together, how they cooperate, and substantially more. This guideline can likewise be applied to families.

All in all, what are relational peculiarities?
The word relational peculiarities alludes to the manners by which relatives interface. Every relative might encounter these elements in an unexpected way, and they may likewise cover and affect each other. For instance, the elements between a mother and father can modify the dynamic of a whole family; in the event that they are not getting along, it can deliver pressure that is felt by all individuals and damages the family all in all. Relational peculiarities are imperative in the development and improvement of every relative, having the ability to adjust the way that they see and connect with the world. Family interactions can likewise affect emotional well-being and prosperity.

Family relationships

Families, in contrast to pants or night wear, don't come in one size fits all. Families are more similar to snowflakes in that no two are exactly the same. Dynamics are the powers that structure and change complex frameworks. In this example, elements are powers that can change what families look like and capability. These relational, social, and social factors can incorporate family size, cosmetics, or customs.

A few families, for instance, eat specific dinners together consistently, however others don't. A few families incorporate aunties, uncles, and grandparents in their living plans, however others pick the family unit structure, which incorporates just guardians and youngsters. Various Dynamics can change the presence of a family, where they live, and which capabilities they have.
We've depicted relational peculiarities as relational, social, and social, yet remember that a few elements might influence others. These associations are confounded and every now and again interlaced.

Certain family dynamic roles can indicate if a family is dysfunctional or healthy. These obligations are attributed to unmistakable relatives and impact how they associate with each other. The jobs effectively keep up with harmony by controlling the assumptions that different individuals have for one another. They can be either certain or adverse, relying upon how they are understood.

Using Influence to Navigate Friendships and Social Circles

Friendship is a pivotal part of life. They furnish us with a feeling of having a place, humor, satisfaction, and everyday encouragement. They are habitually responsible for giving the counsel and understanding that we expect during troublesome minutes. In the event that you have a decent organization of caring people who never keep you on the clouded side of obliviousness, you will constantly have a hopeful outlook on hurrying to them and examining your interests.

Here is my own insight and point of view on companionship and what your gathering means for your own advancement. We've all heard the maxim, "As the organization develops, so does the way of behaving." We are more recognizable by the companions we keep or spend out with after our families. Our partners' mentalities, choices, and propensities are reflected in our own perspectives, choices, and propensities.

In my vocation as an occasion organizer, wedding organizer, vocalist, persuasive orator, writer, organization pioneer, thus considerably more, I've discovered that Friendships can construct, elevate, and reinforce you whenever taken care of with a spotless heart. They can lead you down a course that you shouldn't take.

Future is made by presence.

We often consider the potential episodes that might happen, yet how might we make a superior future on the off chance that we don't live solidly in the present? In our ongoing circumstance, the presence of our self, family, and, in particular, our companions' circle generally affects us. On the off chance that somebody is bamboozled by a companion or lives in a circle that chatters a great deal, that individual will not be able to trust new people, regardless of whether they tell the truth and can be supportive friends.

Having friends who are useful, reliable, and give sound exhortation creates a powerful urge in our own development to make future decisions that are more moderate, created, and equipped for managing current circumstances, whether positive or negative.

A more joyful and better presence

Friendships have a significant effect in different ways. Up to this point, that's what I've found assuming you're encircled by an organization that is brimming with life and energizes dynamic support throughout everyday life and relationships, you'll be learned to do likewise.
I encountered some psychological trouble because of monetary hardships in my day to day existence. Yet, on account of my caring loved ones, I had the option to escape what is happening without risking my psychological or actual wellbeing. This might have all the earmarks of being an unrealistic fantasy, yet it is valid. Individuals who have strong social connections carry on with better and more joyful lives, as indicated by study.

Personal preferences and education

At the point when friends share their playlists, interests, food sources, and dress styles, there is a far and wide impression that a taste comes off on one another. Our Friendships are likewise personally connected with our specific preferences and learning new things. In any event, when I initially began singing, I was propelled by one of my dear companions who used to sing quite a while in the past.

This impact might appear to be immaterial, however it can possibly immensely affect our development and awareness.

How we invest our energy, whether it is through sports, magnanimous work, perusing, or examining thoughts and conclusions with our companions at a party or espresso, is an entirely unexpected opinion.

Within a friend circle, our impression of our choices changes or is marginally impacted.

CHAPTER FIVE

Leadership and Management Influences

Influencing others is a crucial leadership talent. To influence implies to have an impact on the actions, attitudes, views, and decisions of others. Influence isn't equivalent to power or control. It is not about using others to your advantage. It is about knowing what motivates employee dedication and using that information to improve performance and achieve great results.

Trust underpins a leader's ability to influence others; in fact, our influence grows in direct proportion to the level of trust in a connection. Consider how leaders can effectively build trust and influence with others.
Make your credibility known.
Leaders start by establishing credibility in order to build trust.

Credibility is enhanced by integrity, intent, ability, and results. Being truthful and "walking your talk" are examples of integrity. Intent is concerned with making your motivations apparent.

The skills and knowledge required to execute a decent job are referred to as capabilities. What we achieve is our track record—your ability to complete tasks when you say you will.

Building credibility leads to building trust, which is a key step in gaining influence with others.
Engage individuals and make a connection.
Leadership is not a solo act. If you want to have an impact on others, you must involve them. Seek opinions on key decisions that will affect individuals or the team as a whole. Involve employees early in the process of proposing or implementing changes.
Making connections with individuals is another way for leaders to broaden their effect. Seek to understand the needs, motivations, and ideals of people. When you demonstrate a true commitment to what is essential to someone else, you will begin to acquire influence with them because they will recognize that your actions reflect a genuine concern for their interests.

Set clear expectations for yourself and hold yourself accountable.
Leaders must be able to enlist, persuade, and involve others in order to achieve extraordinary results. Leaders, on the other hand, must clearly clarify expectations

before asking staff to commit. Define the results and make them visible to others. Once the findings have been defined, practice accountability. Hold yourself and others accountable for exceeding expectations. When leaders fail to set expectations and enforce accountability, they inadvertently contribute to and create a low-trust environment in which mediocrity is the norm. This has an instant impact on your ability to influence others positively. Extend your excitement

One of the reasons why passion is so important is because it generates energy and ignites others. Passion has a contagious quality. It is impossible to feign enthusiasm. It should be true and real. If a leader doesn't care about a cause, for what reason would it be a good idea for anyone else?

It isn't enough for a leader to have a vision; the individual must likewise have the option to impart that vision and evoke energy and backing from others.

Successful leaders impact others by sharing their fervor and energy.

Be available to be impacted. Impact ought to be equal. One of the most straightforward ways of fortifying your impact with others is to be available to impact yourself. This requires certified transparency. Be available to hearing others' thoughts and welcoming and taking into account contradicting perspectives. Use the abilities and information on others. You will acquire regard and trust from individuals assuming you exhibit transparency, which will build your effect.

Effective leadership Approaches and Styles

The leadership style of a pioneer alludes to how the person coordinates, rouses, and oversees others.
 A person's leadership style determines how they strategize and implement goals while keeping stakeholders' expectations and their team's well-being in mind.

Why Is It Important to Comprehend Your Leadership Style?

Knowing your leadership style enables you to provide effective direction and feedback to employees, as well as a better understanding of your thoughts, decision-making processes, and methods to consider when making company decisions.

It can also help you understand how your direct reports perceive you and why they may make specific comments to you. Employees, for example, may be telling you that you're an autocratic leader who should modify your style if they feel limited at work and don't have many opportunities to express themselves.

Knowing your leadership styles can help you grow even when you receive little criticism. Each leadership style has faults that can be avoided by addressing areas for development early on. This is critical since some employees may be unwilling to speak up, even in an anonymous survey.

Leadership Style Types

1. Democratic Leadership: Sometimes referred to as Facilitative or Participatory Leadership
Democratic leadership is precisely that: the team member's participation is considered when making choices. Each worker has an equal voice in the direction of a project, even though the leader has the final say.

Democratic leaders frequently exhibit the following traits:
- Encouraging

- cooperative
- Strong communicator who empowers
- kind and encouraging
- Establishing trust
- Empathetically knowledgeable

Why firms benefit from this leadership style:

This type of leadership is similar to how executives frequently decide during board meetings.
In a board meeting of the company, for instance, a democratic leader could present the group with a few options for decisions. After that, they might start talking about each choice. Following a discussion, this leader may decide to put the choice to a vote or take into account the opinions and suggestions of the board.

Why the team benefits from this leadership style:

1. Democratic leadership
This is among the most successful because it fosters a culture where everyone feels empowered to voice their thoughts, participate in all processes, and trust that their voices will be heard. Employee engagement is also bolstered by the knowledge that their opinions will be heard.

Employee empowerment, motivation, and involvement can all be increased when team members feel free to contribute.

2. Autocratic Leadership:
Also referred to as Commanding, Authoritarian, or Coercive Leadership
The opposite of democratic leadership is autocratic leadership. Decisions are made by the leader in this method without consulting anyone who reports to them.

Generally speaking, autocratic leadership is defined by:
- Centralized selection of actions
- Top-down and direct communication
- Very little delegation
- Limited independence among team members
- A focus on status and hierarchy
- Averse to criticism or comments

This is not a stand-alone leadership style; rather, it works best when a corporation needs to exert control over particular circumstances. It may work well, for example, in emergency or crisis situations where prompt and decisive action is required.

Why firms benefit from this leadership style:
Autocratic leaders give their full attention to implementing plans and orders. Thus, when circumstances demand it, a strong leader may act quickly to determine what is best for the company without seeking further advice (which can be useful in certain situations).

Why the team benefits from this leadership style:
When a business has to make tough decisions without the benefit of extra advice from people who aren't as knowledgeable as the organization, this kind of leadership works best. In addition to providing workers with a clear sense of direction and authority, responsible parties can compensate for inexperience on a team.

3. Leadership with Laissez-Faire

Also known as: Hands-off or Delegative Leadership
You'll correctly think that laissez-faire leadership is the least invasive style of leadership if you can still recall your high school French. The direct translation of the French phrase "laissez-faire" is "let them do."
Leaders who practice it delegate almost all authority to their staff and hardly speak up unless necessary.

Among the essential traits of laissez-faire leadership are:

- Insufficient direction, guidance, and feedback
- Minimal control and interference
- Great independence and liberty
- Confidence and empowerment

Why firms benefit from this leadership style:
Laissez-faire managers hold staff members responsible for their work. Many workers are encouraged to perform at their highest level by this. A laid-back corporate culture is frequently fostered by this kind of boss. Because of this, it's a useful model for creative industries like product design or advertising companies.
Additionally, a company with a highly skilled workforce might benefit from it.

Why the team benefits from this leadership style:
In a fledgling company for instance, the founder of the company may be a laissez-faire individual who doesn't establish any formal office standards about deadlines or work hours. While they concentrate on the general operations of managing the business, they may have total faith in their staff.
It is this high degree of trust that makes workers under laissez-faire bosses feel important. They

obtain the necessary information, then apply their resources and expertise to achieve their business objectives.

4. Headline Management

A company's growth prospects and main operations are separated by strategic leaders. This kind of leadership calls for adaptability, cutthroat mindfulness, and vision.

While assuming the heaviness of executive interests, these pioneers additionally ensure that every other person's functioning circumstances stay stable.

The objective of an essential leader is to direct their organization toward its drawn out goals. You can assemble an association that is ground breaking, adaptable, and dexterous and that can succeed in the consistently changing business climate of today by utilizing this leadership style.

Why firms benefit from this leadership style:

Plans for development and methodology are connected by essential leaders to group the executives' strategies. They plan for future extension, form and complete systems, and suggest conversation starters. This procedure accomplishes normal business goals like:

- Responsibility

- Efficiency
- Cooperation
- Objectivity

Why the group benefits from this leadership style:
Because of its capacity to help different representative sorts at the same time, essential reasoning makes this a beneficial initiative style for some organizations.

Numerous organizations view vital reasoning as a beneficial style since it upholds different workers without a moment's delay. It can motivate laborers and advance preparation, representation, and boosting the utilization of current assets.

5. Transformational Leadership:

Transformational leaders move colleagues, prevail upon their trust and certainty, and guide staff individuals toward accomplishing hierarchical targets.

Furthermore, Transformational leadership generally upgrades the organization's practices and rouses staff individuals to progress and expand their ranges of abilities.

A Transformational leader's definitive design is to leave a positive inheritance, move their group to arrive at their most noteworthy potential, and drive hierarchical achievement.

Why this leadership style is gainful to businesses:
Transformational leaders can rouse their staff to think in an unexpected way. This can help organizations in refreshing business strategies to build proficiency and benefit. Worker joy, resolve, and inspiration can all profit from it.

Why this leadership style benefits the team:
This is a highly encouraging style of leadership in which people are supported and encouraged to see what they are capable of.

When starting a new work with this type of leader, all employees may be given a list of goals to meet and timeframes to meet them by. Goals may start off basic, but as employees progress and fulfill their objectives, supervisors may assign them more duties and challenges to do as they progress with the organization.

6. Transactional Management

To encourage and direct behavior, transactional leadership employs reward and punishment. These managers establish clear norms and criteria for their personnel and actively monitor their performance. They inform staff that if a target is fulfilled, they will be rewarded.

This leadership style is concerned with preserving the status quo and meeting preset goals and criteria. It also assumes that teams require structure and monitoring to achieve corporate objectives and that they are driven by rewards.

Why this leadership style is beneficial to businesses:
This style is popular in business because it focuses on outcomes, established institutions, and predetermined systems of incentives or penalties. This leadership style also acknowledges and rewards dedication.

Why this leadership style benefits the team:
Transactional leaders can provide useful clarity and framework of expectations, making employees feel comfortable since they understand what is expected of them. Employees also understand what they will receive in exchange for fulfilling corporate objectives.

7. Leadership Coaching
Also known as: Conscious Leadership
A coaching leader focuses on discovering and developing each team member's specific abilities,

as well as establishing tactics to help teams operate better together.

This leadership style is similar to strategic and democratic leadership, but it focuses on the success of individual employees.

A manager with this leadership style may assist people strengthen their abilities by: assigning new tasks to them to try. Providing direction Meeting to discuss constructive criticism

They may also urge one or more team members to broaden their skill set by learning new abilities from their teammates.

Coaching leaders place a premium on developing trust and good relationships with their team members. They promote an environment of open communication and psychological safety, which encourages people to share ideas, get feedback, and collaborate toward common goals.

Why this leadership style is beneficial to businesses:

Coaching leaders actively encourage skill development and problem-solving independence. They achieve ambitious corporate goals by cultivating a strong company culture and contribute to a corporation's long-term vision as vital mentors, frequently even after leaving a company.

Why this leadership style benefits the team:
Employees may be motivated by this leadership style if they feel supported on the team. It recognizes that each individual is unique and can form diverse and fascinating teams in which each employee contributes something unique.

This leader prioritizes excellent performance, employing people who can communicate effectively and embrace diverse skill sets to get the job done.

8. Bureaucratic Management

Bureaucratic leaders adhere to the rules. Unlike authoritarian leaders, they may listen to and consider employee opinion, but they may reject input that contradicts business policy or historical practices.

Some important aspects of bureaucratic leadership are:

- centralized action selection
- Strict adherence to procedures and rules
- There is a clear chain of command.
- Limited independence

Why this leadership style is beneficial to businesses:
This procedure turns out best for bigger, more seasoned, established businesses that are already successful. This leadership style works for these

companies since they need to save their ongoing plans of action and methods since they are fruitful, and taking a stab at anything new that doesn't work could sit around and assets.

Why this leadership style helps the group:
This leadership style might be challenging for some, however it has enormous advantages. It lessens the chance of partiality and replaces it with focal capabilities, work security, and consistency.
For certain individuals, this immediate and viable authority style might bring about elevated degrees of inventiveness.

9. Insightful Leadership
Otherwise called: Affiliative Leadership
Visionary leadership is worried about the future and the long term.
  They want to motivate and guide their team to reach a common goal.
Collaboration, emotional intelligence, and teamwork are all encouraged by this style of leader. They also encourage people to accept new ideas and practices by cultivating an environment of innovation and change.
Why this leadership style is beneficial to businesses:

Visionary leaders can design a clear plan that staff members can follow and carry out. Because they are effective and captivating communicators, they motivate teams to achieve great business success.

Because they are focused on future progress, visionary leaders may predict potential barriers and map out action plans, which instills confidence in their employees amid uncertain or difficult times.
Why this leadership style benefits the team:
When a team has a goal to strive toward, they can accomplish more and enjoy their work more. This type of leader provides vision statements and other resources to motivate team members to participate in their work.

10. Pacesetters in Leadership

A pacesetter sets high expectations and expects employees to meet them exactly as they've indicated. Because they expect high levels of productivity and quality work from their employees, these managers may interfere to ensure tasks are completed precisely and on time.
A pacesetter's characteristics include:
- High performance standards
- Providing a good example
- Result-driven
- Preference for speed and efficiency

Why this leadership style is beneficial to businesses:
This type of leader ensures that employees understand exactly what is expected of them by setting high expectations and focusing on meeting them. Pacesetting sales leaders, for example, set and exceed target quarterly sales cadences.
These leaders may also work with their team to improve performance and enhance team morale.

Why this leadership style is beneficial to the team:
Skilled and experienced teams frequently thrive under this type of leadership. They make meeting goals feel urgent and exciting by utilizing the strengths of motivated and skilled team members.
It can also be uplifting for team members to witness their boss putting in the effort with them.

11. Leadership in Adversity
Situational leaders modify their leadership style to meet the needs of the situation or team. It infers that effective leaders should change their leadership style to fit the degree of arrangement and improvement of their colleagues.
This leadership style involves inspecting explicit occasions, assessing people's skill and responsibility, and changing the main system

likewise. It is proactive and recognizes that the main steady change is.

Why this leadership style is viable in business: This leadership methodology can move staff and guarantee that they are not compelled to work in manners that are unseemly for the situation. It's particularly valuable for new companies or organizations that require continuous changes as well as adaptable labor force and help.

Why this leadership style helps the group:
Situational pioneers are great communicators who pursue choices in light of group criticism. They additionally screen market drifts and may rapidly survey and change strategies to guarantee a good outcome. This can be a major area of strength for cultivating and helping representatives get it and value their worth to the organization.

How can collaboration and teamwork be enhanced through the use of persuasion?
You might not consider persuasion to be a collaborative and teamwork-related skill. Persuasion is crucial in teamwork situations as well as when speaking with supervisors, clients, vendors, and possible business partners. Your persuasive abilities can come in handy when

working with others in a team in two very different ways: they can inspire others to give their all and they can assist you in working with colleagues to reach wise conclusions.

Causes of change resistance
According to their research on resistance to change theory, there are four typical circumstances in which people become resistant to change:

- Personal gain
- Miscommunication and a lack of confidence
- disparate assessments
- Low capacity to adapt

We may observe the development of many forms of resistance to change by using our example of change.

1. Self-centeredness
Someone is likely to oppose a change if they think they might lose something important as a result of it. People prioritize their personal goals over the organization's best interests since each stakeholder has a different agenda. This in the end transforms into a hesitance to change among the group.

2. A lack of confidence and misinterpretation

Another factor contributing to resistance to change is ignorance of the consequences of the change. This miscommunication is made worse by the manager's lack of trust with the employees who are supposed to carry out the changes.

3. Differing assessments

People who evaluate the effects of transformation differently than their supervisors or other change initiators find themselves in this scenario.

4. A poor ability to adapt

Some people are afraid of change because they think they won't be able to acquire the necessary skills and abilities. This is especially true for projects that call for quick changes—people find it more difficult to adjust to changes that are larger and occur more quickly.

Six techniques to get through change-resistant people

Organizations need to work in six main areas when it comes to tactics and techniques for lowering resistance to change.

1. Instruction and communication

Common problems that lead to resistance to change include ignorance of the reasons behind change's necessity and fear of the unknown.

Only when the risk of staying the same exceeds the risk of going in a different direction will people accept change. In a similar vein, individuals will wonder why you are changing something they think is effective if they don't see why change is necessary.

It is best to start educating people and communicating about the change before it is implemented. This will guarantee that teams and individuals have enough knowledge to make informed decisions and assist your workers in justifying the change.

2. Incorporation

Resistance to change stems from a lack of confidence in the organization's ability to implement changes successfully. Similar to this, resistance is probably going to be stronger when people are being forced to change without their consent. This is particularly true if individuals think their careers are under jeopardy.

Involving stakeholders and change implementers in the design process is essential. People will be involved in the transformation and in identifying possible problems and solutions through cooperative efforts. When people have contributed to the change, they are much less inclined to oppose it.

Utilizing socialization—which prioritizes people over practice and makes sure that resistance to change is crushed by shared values—is another participative method.

3. Support Routines

Are typically changed in conjunction with organizational transformation, forcing individuals out of their (long-established) comfort zones. Additionally, this could result in fatigue, particularly if the company has regular changes or corporate advancements.

People might just be resigned to change, even if they seem to be receptive to it. In order to facilitate the development of new abilities and prevent change burnout, they must be provided with the necessary support.

4. Concurrence

People become resistant to change when they believe the changes will have a negative impact on them. This can be because of a belief that the benefits of the change won't outweigh the work needed, or that their income or professional prospects would suffer.

An organization can think about providing incentives in order to overcome this kind of resistance to change. These incentives could come in the form of more income, better perks, or career goals that are structured. To obtain an agreement using this method, bargaining is necessary. The disadvantage is that these contracts don't ensure that people will embrace change and can be costly.

5. Co-opting

People grow attached to the established manner of doing things. Employees may have contributed to the development of processes and procedures, for which there are frequently significant emotional ties. It can take a herculean effort to form a bond with the elderly.

Putting those who might be the most opposed to change in key positions during the execution of change projects is one tactic. This can garner the support of potential opponents at a relatively low cost, but there is a catch: putting those who are thought to be resistant to change in these kinds of roles may provide them with a platform from which to inspire more resistance among a larger audience.

6. Forced labor

People may need to be forced to embrace change at times. This is frequently the case when people believe change is just a passing trend that will be abandoned or when they believe they are incapable of learning the new skills required.

Using the fear of disciplinary action as a tool to get people to comply with necessary behaviors and activities is one way to accomplish change. Coercion might be the only practical solution if the rate of change is crucial.

CHAPTER SIX

Moral Aspects of Influence

Some contend that a business's primary goal should be to maximize profits and that it would be against fiduciary responsibility to concentrate on any other issues. However, being in the highly competitive sphere of business does not need an organization to be immoral. It is still possible for a firm to generate a profit and maintain moral standards in its operations. Given the growing influence of social media on a company's reputation, any corporation that steers clear of moral blunders will improve its reputation and attract a devoted following of customers who share its values, which will increase sales and profits.

The truth should be stated, customers should be treated with respect, and both sides to a transaction should be handled fairly in order for them to gain from it jointly are basic principles that your business should abide by. An ethical money-making company strategy should be established and followed because a moral business can only prosper if it is profitable.

Identifying Manipulative Influence Techniques

When someone engages in gaslighting, love bombing, or other manipulative relationship tactics in an effort to obtain control or influence over another, it is referred to as manipulative behavior. Attempts to harm the emotional and mental health of another person are frequently included in these strategies. Although manipulation is more likely in firmly knit relationships, it can occur in casual or close relationships as well. It covers any effort to manipulate someone's feelings in order to influence how they behave or feel.

Indications of Deception

There are several ways that manipulation can occur. In actuality, depending on the goal, being nice can be a kind of manipulation.

You can search for several common qualities in those who manipulate other people. They consist of:

- They are adept at taking advantage of your shortcomings.
- They take advantage of your weaknesses.
- They persuade you to give up something valuable in order to increase your reliance on them.

If they are successful in manipulating you, they will keep doing so until you leave the circumstance. Talented employees may be sent by a manipulator to the local employment agency in search of employment. They incite conflict, set themselves up for failure, and exacerbate already tense professional relationships. Projects are ruined, deadlines are missed, the emotional atmosphere is drastically altered, coworkers are treated horribly, and individuals are kept unhappy for as long as they choose by manipulators. They rely on others' discretion and good intentions, as well as on concealment.

Maintaining Honesty While Seeking to Persuade Others

Being morally clear-headed, honest, and ethical are traits of integrity. And being honest and respectful are just two aspects of integrity at work. Trustworthy Employees that work for an organization with a veritable culture view their undertakings in a serious way, step up when they don't have the foggiest idea what they should do, and at last get a sense of ownership with their activities. Consequently, the company prospers.

Describe integrity

Being morally upright and honest are qualities of integrity. Even when things are private, an ethical person acts morally and does the right thing.

Two instances of displaying integrity in regular situations are telling the clerk that you were given too much change or returning to the store to pay for an item you forgot to pay for.

Seven characteristics of integrity

Integrity could appear to be an ill-defined term. You might need a more precise definition if you wish to promote integrity at work and practice it yourself.

The following are the top 7 characteristics of an honest person:
- Being thankful for other people
- Esteeming transparency and honesty
- Accepting Responsibility and duty for all of your acts, both good and bad
- Honoring oneself and those around you, wherever you may be
- Giving to the less fortunate without compromising your own well-being
- Proving to be dependable and trustworthy

- Remaining calm and adaptable in the face of unforeseen challenges

Integrity at work is really about taking the initiative, being truthful in your time negotiation, and maintaining alignment between your personal and professional ideals. This also entails keeping your word when you make commitments and declining more tasks when you are unable to do so. Ultimately, it comes down to communication skills. If you do err, you should be able to own up to your faults and explain how you plan to put things right.

When you arrive at work on time and exhibit reliability,you are considered trustworthy especially when handling sensitive material and high-risk assignments.

Engage in and promote candid conversation with bosses and coworkers.

Show consideration, integrity, and patience to coworkers, supervisors, and clients.

Possess a strong work ethic and make it your goal to regularly generate high-quality work

are accountable for your deeds, particularly when you commit an error

Make wise choices even in stressful circumstances.

Are prepared to offer your clients excellent service.

Describe Business Ethics.

In regards to potentially contentious topics including corporate governance, insider trading, bribery, discrimination, corporate social responsibility, fiduciary responsibilities, and much more, business ethics examines ethical business rules and practices. Business ethics frequently follow the law, but they can also serve as a fundamental set of rules that companies can go by to win over the public.

The Fundamentals of Business Ethics
It's critical to comprehend the moral standards that underpin desirable ethical behavior and how many otherwise brilliant and talented individuals—as well as the companies they represent—fail due to a lack of these moral standards.

Generally speaking, these are some corporate ethical guidelines:

- Leadership: The deliberate attempt to embrace, incorporate, and model the remaining 11 principles to direct choices and actions in all spheres of one's personal and professional life.
- Accountability: Taking responsibility for your own and other people's actions. a dedication

to upholding moral principles and making sure others do the same.

- Integrity: Contains the following principles: reliability, honesty, and trustworthiness. A person with integrity always tries to do the right thing and raises the bar for themselves.

- Respect for others: Treating people with respect is essential to promoting moral behavior and work cultures. Everyone is entitled to respect, privacy, equality, opportunity, kindness, and understanding.

- Honesty: Promoting an ethical atmosphere requires telling the truth in all regards. Omissions, understatement or overstatement, and partial truths do not assist a company in increasing its performance. In order to find solutions, bad news should be shared and received in the same way as good news.

- Respect for the law: Upholding all municipal, state, and federal laws is a crucial part of ethical leadership. Leaders should err on the side of legality rather than taking advantage of a legal loophole if there is one.

- Transparency: Those with an interest in a business, including shareholders, staff, the community in which the company operates, and the families of staff members, are considered stakeholders.

- Compassion: It is important to show concern for the welfare of employees, clients, partners in business, and the community in which a company operates. Companies should make sure information about their financials, price changes, hiring and firing practices, wages and salaries, and promotions is available to those interested in the business's success, without disclosing trade secrets.

- Fairness: This requires that everyone be treated similarly and given equal opportunities.
A practice or conduct is probably unfair if it makes you uncomfortable or prioritizes corporate or personal gain over equality, decency, and respect.

- Loyalty: Executives should be devoted to the company and its workers, and they should act in confidence. Encouraging fidelity among staff members and supervisors guarantees their dedication to optimal procedures.

- Environmental concern: It is crucial to be aware of and worried about the environmental effects a business has in a world where resources are few, ecosystems have been harmed by prior actions, and the climate is changing. It should be encouraged of all employees to identify and report procedures that may compound already-done harm.

Why Is Ethics in Business Important?

Business ethics are crucial for success in the modern business world for a number of reasons. The main advantage of determined morals programs is that they make a general set of rules that directs the way of behaving of all staff individuals, including chiefs, center directors, and passage level laborers. A company's reputation for ethical behavior is established when all of its personnel make moral decisions. It gains recognition and starts to enjoy the advantages that a moral establishment has to offer:

- Growth and awareness of the brand
- Enhanced capacity for bargaining Enhanced confidence in goods and services
- Growth and retention of customers
- Draws in talent and investments

All of these elements work together to influence a company's earnings. Those who fall short establish and uphold moral norms.

How to Put Ethics in Business Practice

It takes time and work to cultivate an atmosphere of moral behavior and judgment; the highest levels always take the lead. To enforce ethical behavior, the majority of businesses must develop guiding principles, reporting mechanisms, training programs, and a code of conduct or ethics.

Following the definition of behavior and the implementation of programs, ongoing employee communication becomes essential. Leaders should always urge staff members to report suspicious activity and provide guarantees that those who do so won't face retaliation.

CONCLUSION

One of the most important tasks a leader faces is influencing others. " Oxford Languages defines influence as "the ability to have an effect on the character, development, or behavior of someone or something, or the effect itself."

What gets in the way of your ability to make changes or find solutions within your organization? Sometimes the problem facing new managers isn't a lack of experience, expertise, or time; rather, it's their incapacity to win over a more senior executive. Whether it's taking care of a culture conflict or implementing a fresh project for your group, you may know exactly what has to be done, but your supervisor isn't on board. They are, at best, indifferent, and, at worst, very hard to persuade.

You may exert enough influence to bring about significant change in your organization by taking the initiative, posing the correct questions, problem-solving alongside decision-makers, and convincing them of the worth and advantages of a solution. In the event that your supervisor ends up changing your opinion, that will cultivate a relationship of mutual influenceability, which is a potent force for cooperation.

An essential set of abilities for any leader is the ability to influence others. They can assist you in motivating your employees or coworkers to hear your ideas in order to accomplish departmental or corporate goals. Depending on your role, influencing abilities can encourage cooperation among subordinates under your supervision and inspire them to give projects you give them their all. Improving your influencing abilities could increase your chances of getting selected for a leadership role if you aren't already in one.

Use these abilities to convince your manager to take a look at your suggestions for increasing sales or cutting expenses, for example. Your supervisor will also perceive your leadership potential when you apply these newly developed talents.

Why is it crucial for managers to have influence?
Because of their positive vibes and excitement, a lot of successful people in leadership positions draw others to them. In the workplace, their ability to influence others can be determined by how

likable they are. Influence in a managerial position is crucial for a number of reasons:

- Influence encourages staff growth.Your team members may be more inclined to grow naturally in their professions via perseverance and hard work if they regard you as someone they like and would like to impress.
- Results are accelerated by influence. Encourage your staff to go above and beyond expectations by using positive reinforcement to motivate them when you want to see improved output or outcomes from them.
- A productive work atmosphere is produced by influence. Setting a good example and giving it your all could inspire your group since others might wish to emulate your passion and work ethic.